Nobodies for Jesus

14 Days Toward a Great Commission Lifestyle

Chuck Lawless

Published by Rainer Publishing
www.rainerpublishing.com

ISBN 978-0615960890

Printed in the United States of America

To

Brother Jack Tichenor, who consistently modeled
evangelism for me

and

to my wife Pam, whose faithful service for Christ
consistently challenges me

Contents

Introduction 1

Be Amazed

Day 1 Be Amazed at the Master's Power 7
Day 2 Be Amazed at the Master's Uniqueness 13
Day 3 Be Amazed at His Humility 20
Day 4 Be Amazed at His Surprising Love 27
Day 5 Be Amazed at His Forgiving Grace 33
Day 6 Be Amazed that He Uses Us Anyway 39

Be a Nobody

Day 7 Be a Nobody: Let Go of Your Name 46
Day 8 Be a Nobody: Get over
Your Achievements 53
Day 9 Be a Nobody: Beware of Greatness 60
Day 10 Be a Nobody: Be Honest about
Your Sin 67
Day 11 Be a Nobody: Be Willing to be Broken 74
Day 12 Be a Nobody: Give Up Self for
Non-Believers 80

Do Something

Day 13   Do Something: Pray God's
             Heart for the World   88

Day 14   Do Something: Tell Your Story   94

Conclusion   101

Introduction

I am a professor of evangelism and missions in a time when evangelicals aren't doing much evangelism. In my own denomination, we are reporting fewer baptisms than we did five decades ago. I teach missions in a time when 1.7 billion people still have little or no access to the gospel. We have resources like seldom before, but still the church is failing to do the work of the Great Commission. Something must change.

I don't think, however, that new programs are the answer. I'm not opposed to programs, but programs by themselves have proven to be a failure. Many programs for developing a Great Commission church begin by training church members to do evangelism – but I'm convinced that's not always the best direction.

The problems are several. First, many of us have lost our first love for Christ (Rev. 2:4). Our passion that first drove us to tell the good news dissipated long ago. Our faith has become more intellectual assent than childlike wonder.

Second, we don't see people as sheep without a shepherd; we fail to have compassion on the crowds (Matt. 9:36). The crowds are just that – crowds – anonymous and numerous. Even our neighbors are unknown to us. The lost nations of the world grab our attention only when the cable networks bring them to mind. While our enemy wants to keep the world in darkness (2 Cor. 4:3-4), the church has become a place to retreat from the world rather than a place to re-arm for the battle.

Here's the premise that underlies this book: lukewarm believers who fail to see people as lost will not be Great Commission believers. We will not be God's force set apart to make a dent in the darkness of the world.

We will go through the motions of Christianity without seeing life transformation. We will be who we are . . . and that alarms me. Again, I say, something must change.

I thank you for joining me in this study, and I want to give you directions about where we're headed together in this study. First, this study is intensely biblical. I start with the assumption that the Bible is God's inspired Word, cutting us to the bone even as it equips us for holy living (Heb 4:12; 2 Tim. 3:16-17). I make no apology for grounding this study in the Word of God.

Second, our goal is to grow in commitment and obedience to the Great Commission. Five times in the New Testament (Matt. 28:18-20, Mark 16:15, Luke 24:45-49, John 20:21, Acts 1:8), Jesus echoed the words most often quoted from Matthew 28:

> All authority has been given to Me in heaven and on earth. Go, therefore, and make disciples of all nations, baptizing them in the name of the Father and of the Son and of the Holy Spirit, teaching them to observe everything I have commanded you. And remember, I am with you always, to the end of the age.

Five times Jesus told us to do this. Apparently, the Great Commission was important to him. Our responsibility as believers is to teach the good news to our families, to our neighbors, to our nation, and to the world. Every one of us has both the privilege and responsibility to do the Great Commission – but many of us leave that responsibility to our paid church staff and other leaders. A dying world will never be won to Christ if only our church staff members are doing the work. I trust that this study will lead you to find *your* place in doing the Great Commission.

Admittedly, this book is brief. It does not cover all you need to develop a Great Commission lifestyle, but that's not the point of this work. I want you to return to wonder and amazement over Jesus – and consequently, to pull away from self. I am convinced those steps are critical in moving toward being a Great Commission believer.

This book is designed for you to study three general topics over fourteen days: "Be Amazed," "Be a Nobody," and "Do Something." Each daily reading concludes with reflection questions and a guided prayer to help you apply the teachings for that day. In addition, each day includes a simple "Great Commission Action Step" to help you move toward a Great Commission lifestyle from the first day of this study. My goal is to keep the readings short while allowing the Word of God to penetrate our hearts. The daily work should require no more than thirty minutes, though I trust that the readings will reverberate in your heart and mind all day.

Let's do this together, for that's the only way that God's church will accomplish the Great Commission. When God grabs your heart somewhere in this study, rest in that divine moment. When he challenges you to the point of discomfort, know that he has a Great Commission purpose in mind. Press on faithfully when the enemy tempts you to end this study early. And, if you do stop early and put this book on the shelf, pick it up again.

 I pray that the approach in this study leads you to genuine lifestyle change rather than just a program's completion. Here I use the word "pray" literally, as I will be praying for individuals and groups that use this study. I may not know your name, but God does – and he wants you to be a Great Commission Christian. I also assume that your group, if you are reading with a group, will be praying intentionally for each other.

So, that's where we're headed. Only fourteen days. Fourteen life-changing days, I hope. Get your Bible and a pen, and let's go. Prepare to become a nobody for Jesus.

Be Amazed

"Give us a church that loves Jesus Christ much. You will have mighty prayer-meetings; you will have a holy membership; you will have liberal giving to the cause of Christ; you will have hearty praising of his name; you will have careful walking before the world; you will have earnest endeavours for the conversion of sinners. Missions at home and abroad will be set on foot when love is fervent."

--Charles Spurgeon, 19th century pastor

"The spirit of Christ is the spirit of missions. The nearer we get to Him, the more intensely missionary we become."

--Henry Martyn, 18th and 19th century missionary

Be Amazed at the Master's Power

Text: Mark 4:35-5:43

I just did a Google search on the question, "What do people believe about Jesus?" Some of the responses would be comical if they were not so tragically wrong. Listen to a few of them:

"He was a rabble rouser and good, smart guy who lived and died about 2000 years ago."

"Jesus is not the answer. He is the problem."

"He displayed all the emotions and failings we attribute to mortal beings. He was just a man."

"Was Jesus a God? NO, I do not think so. I believe that Jesus was a very old (advanced) soul that came to earth with advanced knowledge and abilities."

I read these responses, and I get frustrated, if not angry (in what I hope is a God-pleasing way...). I know that Jesus is more than just a man, and he is undoubtedly more than "a very old soul." I have taught for over thirty years that he is the Son of God. I am haunted by this question, though: does my life really show that I believe Jesus is the Son of God? Or, to ask this question more pointedly, *"Am I so amazed by Jesus that I can't help but tell others about him?"*

Take some time now and read (or re-read) today's scripture text. It is a longer selection, but look specifically at how Jesus and the situations he confronted are portrayed in these verses. The picture is really quite powerful.

In the first story, Jesus was the master over nature. A storm was raging – fierce winds blowing, waves breaking over the boat, water swamping the vessel, and seasoned fishermen fearing for their lives. The descriptions are so numerous because the writer wants us to know that this situation was rapidly deteriorating. Meanwhile, Jesus slept (because, of course, he was not worried).

When he was awakened, he spoke to the angry sea. "Silence! Be still!" from the lips of the one who created nature in the first place brought instantaneous calm to the waves and the wind. His disciples could only wonder in amazement, "Who then is this? Even the wind and the sea obey him!" This was not the last time that Jesus would amaze somebody.

In the second story, Jesus was the master over demons. Having come to the other side of sea, Jesus and his disciples confronted a demon-possessed man. The Bible again wants us to know that this man was seriously under the influence of evil powers. He lived in the cemetery. No man could control him, even with chains. His screeches echoed through the mountains. Perhaps in unsuccessful attempts to end his life, he continually cut himself with stones. His demons were almost uncountable.

They were, though, no equal to Jesus. They knew that he was Jesus, Son of the Most High God, and they recognized that he would determine their destiny. He spoke, the demons fled, and the crazed man was miraculously freed. He who calmed the violent sea had now calmed the raging heart of a human being.

In the third story, Jesus was the master over sickness. This story is so powerful that we will look at it in more detail in a later study. A woman had a blood disease for twelve years, and no physician had been able to help her. You know the pattern by now – the writer doesn't want us to miss her desperation:

> "[She] *had endured much* under many doctors. She *had spent everything* she had and *was not helped at all*. On the contrary, *she became worse*." (Mark 5:26, emphasis added)

Can you imagine her grief? Read the text one more time. She had endured much. She spent everything that she had. She was not helped at all. She just became worse. Her life must have descended into a cycle of defeat, despair, discouragement, and depression.

Everything changed, though, when she touched Jesus. Instantly, Jesus did what no doctor could do in over a decade: he healed her disease. Her bleeding dried up, her body was restored, and her soul was made whole. Sickness had met its match; He who was the master over nature and demons was also the master over disease.

In the fourth story, Jesus was the master over death. Jairus' daughter was at the point of death, and he pleaded with Jesus to come heal her. Jesus and a large crowd moved quickly in that direction, knowing that an emergency waited in Jairus' home. The drama and the desperation were only heightened when Jesus stopped to talk to the woman with the blood disease – talking to her so long that word arrived that Jairus' daughter had died. Death had come to Jairus' home before Jesus did.

By this point, we should know that even death would not be a problem for Jesus. Death had ruled the world since the Garden of Eden, but no more. The one who was the way, the truth, and the life (John 14:6) was now on the scene. He spoke to the daughter, and she arose at His command. The master over nature, demons, and sickness was also the master over the final enemy: death. Luke tells us that her parents were, not surprisingly, astounded (Luke 8:56).

Now, go back to the story of the demon-possessed man. Did you catch what happened at the end of that story? The changed man wanted to stay with Jesus (and who wouldn't?), but Jesus would not allow him. Instead, Jesus commissioned him to go back to his home and be a witness of God's mercy. The result when he told his story? Look at it again in verse 20: "they were all amazed."

That's the way the Great Commission works: believers who are amazed by Jesus tell others, and they in turn are amazed. When we lose our amazement, however, our Great Commission passion disappears.

Be honest. As you begin this study, are you amazed at Jesus and his power?

Reflection Questions

1. Reflect on the time that Jesus saved you. What amazed you about him then?
2. If your wonder of Jesus has lessened over time, what do you think has contributed to this decline?
3. List as many reasons as you can to be amazed by Jesus again.

Great Commission Action Step: Today, send an email or a letter to two friends, telling them how amazing Christ has been in your life. Get in the practice of speaking good words about Christ.

Prayer: "Father, forgive me if my amazement over your Son is not as strong as it should be. Help me to see Him again as the Master over all. Amen."

Be Amazed at the Master's Uniqueness

Text: Mark 1:40-45, 5:43

I was not raised in a Christian home. I first heard about Christ when God planted in my seventh-grade classroom a crazy, fanatical twelve-year-old Pentecostal preacher who made it his goal to win me to the Lord that year. His approach was simple: he met me at the classroom door each morning and told me, "Chuck, it's a good thing you lived through the night." He would then continue, "If you hadn't, you'd be in hell. *But* . . . you can receive Jesus into your heart right now."

His technique was not the best, but somewhere in the midst of that message God drove truth into my heart—and my life has never been the same. I remember being so overwhelmed that I loudly emphasized all the words in "Amazing grace, how sweet the sound" the first time I sang this great hymn.

Everything, in fact, was amazing. The songs were amazing. The believers were amazing. The preaching was amazing. My Sunday school class was amazing. The fellowship meals were amazing. Even the church bus that picked me up on Sunday morning seemed amazing.

Do you remember those days?

As much as anything, I remember the Bible's being amazing. I had never heard of Adam and Eve before my conversion, and the story of creation was fascinating. The first time I saw a rainbow after reading Genesis 9, I stared in wonder at the multi-colored reminder of God's promises. The stories of David and Saul so grabbed me that I found it difficult to do anything but read the Bible.

The Old Testament was captivating (well, at least most of it . . .), but nothing caught my attention like the stories of Jesus. Listen to how the people responded to Jesus in the first chapters of the Gospel of Mark, including the stories we studied yesterday:

> "They were astonished at his teaching because,
> unlike the scribes, He was teaching them
> as one having authority." (1:22)

"They were all amazed, so they began to argue with one another, 'What is this? A new teaching with authority! He commands even the unclean spirits, and they obey Him.'" (1:27)

"When evening came, after the sun had set, they began bringing to Him all those who were sick and those who were demon-possessed. The whole town was assembled at the door." (1:32-34)

"When He entered Capernaum again after some days, it was reported that He was at home. So many people gathered together that there was no more room, not even in the doorway, and He was speaking the message to them." (2:1-2)

"As a result, they were all astounded and gave glory to God, saying, 'We have never seen anything like this!'" (2:12b)

"Jesus departed with His disciples to the sea, and a great multitude followed from Galilee, Judea, Jerusalem, Idumea, beyond the Jordan, and around Tyre and Sidon. The great multitude came to Him because they heard about everything He was doing." (3:7-8)

"Who then is this? Even the wind and the sea obey Him!" (4:41)

"So he [the demon-possessed man now changed] went out and began to proclaim in the Decapolis how much Jesus had done for him, and they were all amazed." (5:20)

It's hard to read these texts and not hear common themes. Great multitudes. The whole town. No more room. People everywhere. They were astonished. Amazed. Astounded. They had never seen anything like this.

Hear it again: *they had never seen anything like this*. Jesus was not like anyone else.

But, our primary Bible reading for today sounds quite different from this summary of texts listed above. In today's reading, Jesus told a healed leper and Jairus' family *not* to tell others what He had done. His reasons for this different approach might have been several. He wanted to be known as the source of good news more than as a wonderworker. He knew that crowds coming to him only for miracles might well miss his purpose – or get in the way of others who wanted to hear. Maybe the reason was as simple as His divine time for revealing who He was had not yet come. Whatever the reason for his commands, His instructions were hardly unclear.

You know what happened, though. The leper went out and spread the news so widely that Jesus could no longer visit towns openly. We can't be sure who proclaimed the news of the raising of Jairus' daughter, but we do know their response was the same: "this news spread throughout that whole area" (Matt. 9:26). Catch the irony here: Jesus told them not to tell, and yet they did; He has told us to tell, and yet we often do not. Strange, isn't it?

Without condoning their disobedience to Jesus' commands, surely we understand why the leper and Jairus' family proclaimed their good news. After all, how do you keep secret a cleansing from leprosy and a resurrection from the dead? How do you *not* tell others? They were so amazed by their encounter with Jesus that they could not keep the news to themselves – even when Jesus told them otherwise.

As I finish writing these first two studies, I am again amazed like I was as a young believer. But, I write these words more as confession than as a proclamation. What amazes me now is that I am not *always* amazed at Jesus.

Perhaps I think too much of myself. Maybe – just maybe – my wonder over Jesus decreases as my wonder over self increases. People who think they are somebody seldom stand in amazement at somebody else.

What further amazes me is that Jesus forgives my lack of wonder and lets me start again with a renewed sense of astonishment. He's unique that way.

How can I help but tell the world about him?

Reflection Questions

1. Re-read the texts about Jesus listed in today's study, and circle words that speak of wonder and amazement. Quietly focus on the response of the people.

2. Answer "true" (T), "false" (F), or "uncertain" (U) about each of these statements.

_____ I tell others about Jesus often.

_____ I'm so amazed at Jesus that I'm ready to go anywhere to tell others about him.

_____ I have lost my wonder about Jesus.

3. When was the last time that you told somebody about Jesus?

Great Commission Action Step: Yesterday, you sent an email or a letter to tell someone about the wonder of Jesus. Today, take a risk to *tell* someone about that wonder. You might start with a believer, but then dare to speak to a non-believer as well.

Prayer: "Father, forgive me for not speaking about you. Through this study, please restore my wonder about Christ. Amen."

Be Amazed at His Humility

Text: Philippians 2:5-11, Matthew 28:20

Every December, we tell the story. Jesus, the Son of God, came to earth.   God humbled Himself, took on flesh, and lived among us. We mark that miracle with manger scenes in our yards and stars atop our Christmas trees. Such a story demands celebration, and celebrate we do -- at least on Christmas Day. For one day, we pause briefly to consider God's coming, and then daily life grabs our attention again.

It's not surprising that we seldom focus on the Christmas story beyond that day. The story is a story of self-denying, godly humility, and we are uncomfortable with that topic. Humility, you see, is a no-win subject for us.

If we admit that we're not humble, we can be certain that God is not pleased.   Should we claim to be humble, though, we have already started down the slippery slope of arrogance.   To speak (or write) about humility so that others might learn can itself become a prideful act.

This makes the Christmas story that much more amazing. Read these incredible words that an angel spoke to a distraught young man whose fiancée was unexpectedly pregnant:

> "She will give birth to a son, and you are to name Him Jesus . . . see, the virgin will become pregnant and give birth to a son, and they will name Him Immanuel, which is translated, 'God with us.'"

Immanuel. God with us. The Creator living among the created. The Eternal One in human flesh. Deity in a manger. God himself had come.

Be amazed for a minute.

We cannot fully grasp the miracle behind this story. Our Bible text for today tells us that Jesus existed in the form of God and was equal to God before His coming to earth. He always has been, and always will be, God. He always has been, and always will be, worthy of all praise and deserving of all honor.

The name "Immanuel" surely fits then – Jesus was indeed God with us.

Yet, read again what Christ did. The writer of Philippians piles up the images because he wants us to focus here. Jesus "emptied himself," or made himself nothing. He assumed the very nature of a servant. He became a human being. He humbled Himself. Only God could humble himself and not become arrogant about His humility.

As a human being, Christ grew tired and thirsty (John 4:6-7). He hungered for food (Matt. 4:2). He became troubled in His spirit (John 13:21), even to the point of death (Matt. 26:38). Sorrow so consumed him at times that He prayed with loud cries and tears (Heb. 5:7). It was through suffering that he grew in maturity and uncompromised obedience (Heb. 5:8-9). He was even tempted in all ways like we are (Heb. 4:15). "God with us" was *genuinely* with us in his life. That's humbling.

More specifically, though, Philippians says that Jesus was willing to die on a *cross*, a painful, shameful death reserved for criminals and slaves. The passersby ridiculed him, criminals mocked him, and his murderers gambled for his clothing. Even his own followers had deserted him in fear. From the "form of God" to a lonely "death on a cross" – you cannot be more humbled than that! Humiliated, in fact. "God with us" died there.

This, though, was God's plan. In some mysterious way, Jesus bore our sins on the cross (Isa. 53:6, 12) and paid the penalty for our sin (Rom. 6:23). God, who is absolutely holy, poured out on Jesus his anger over our sin, with the result that his anger toward us was abated (1 John 2:2, 4:10). Think about it—God put on his own son the anger that we so deserve. Christ became a curse for us so we would not be cursed anymore (Gal. 3:13). The story just gets more astounding.

Many years ago, I visited a rocky hillside in Jerusalem that some scholars believe is the site of Jesus' crucifixion. On this hillside were three trees that reminded me of the crosses at Jesus' death, and in front of the hill was a busy bus station. A stench of diesel fuel hung in the air. The loud hum of old bus engines was compounded by a continual chorus of horns blowing in the traffic. What seemed like thousands of people speaking multiple languages stood in the station, waiting for transportation to take them to nowhere important.

A young believer at the time, I stood as quietly and respectfully as I could as I looked toward the trees growing on that small hill. "Here Jesus died for *me*," I thought, "and I can't believe that everyone is ignoring this place. How do people just drive by this holy place as if nothing happened here?" Years later, I have sadly learned that I, too, can get so busy with life that I inadvertently wander past the cross as if it didn't happen. My arrogance sometimes prevents me from seeing his humility.

When we miss his humility in his life and death, we also cannot fully appreciate his exaltation in Philippians 2:9-11. He was God who humbly died in human flesh – yet he will be highly exalted in the end. Not all will follow him, but all will ultimately recognize that he is the Lord. In the meantime, we are responsible to proclaim to the entire world the good news that God has come to us.

Take time now to review Matthew 28:20b again: "And remember, I am with you always, to the end of the age." Do you hear a phrase that has echoed throughout today's study? Jesus told us to make disciples, but He also promised he would be with us always. Indeed, this phrase serves as bookends to Matthew's Gospel: "God with us" (1:27) will always be with us (28:20) as we proclaim the gospel and make disciples.

Make this truth personal. *God came to be with you.* He humbled himself to walk in your footsteps and to die your death. In a twist on humility that is beyond our understanding, God's Son became a baby that he might be exalted as King of kings. *And,* he goes with you wherever he sends you.

That's amazing.

Reflection Questions

1. Why is it so difficult to be humble?
2. Where are you most challenged by today's study?
3. Who in your life needs to hear that the baby Jesus is also the King of kings and Lord of lords?

Great Commission Action Step: Humbly plan a surprise "Christmas in (<u>whatever month it is</u>)," and send gifts to friends who need to know about Jesus. Make sure that the gospel story is attached – and that your friends know that your goal is to tell them about Christ.

Prayer: "Father, I am amazed that your Son came to earth for me. Help me to celebrate this truth every day of the year. Amen."

Learning Humility from Jesus

1. Point away from self.
2. Serve others.
3. Reject the world's offers of recognition.
4. Be willing to die for others.

Be Amazed at His Surprising Love

Text: John 4:1-29, 39-42

There is nothing quite like a country music love song. Sometimes the lyrics are almost silly, but still they draw you in to listen and sing along. Maybe you recognize the lyrics to this country song (and if you do, I suspect you'll be humming the tune the rest of the day):

"They say time takes its toll on a body
Makes the young girl's brown hair turn grey
But honey, I don't care,
I ain't in love with your hair
And if it all fell out, well, I'd love you anyway . . ."

When the chorus resounds with "I'm gonna love you forever . . . forever and ever, amen," even the toughest listener will be moved. There's just something about a forever kind of love expressed in a country song.

Today's Bible reading is about a "forever" kind of love – though it might be difficult to see with the first reading of the text. In some ways, this love is a surprising kind of "forever" love.

Here's the story. It was likely in the heat of the day, when few others would be around, that a Samaritan woman went to the well to draw water. She wanted to see no one, for her town had surely ridiculed and rejected her for her immoral living. You see, she had been married five times and was living with a sixth man. Even by today's loose standards, this woman had crossed the line.

To her surprise, though, there was somebody there. A man. A Jewish man. A Jewish man who was thirsty. A thirsty Jewish man who had something eternal to offer to her.

Most surprisingly, the man spoke to her. Even she knew how strange this was. Jewish men seldom spoke to women in public, and certainly not to a Samaritan woman. She was a half-breed at best, the offspring of Jews and their conquerors from years past. Good Jewish men avoided women like this. Jesus, though, never let cultural customs and prejudices get in the way of His love.

"Give me a drink," he said to her – and then he offered her a different kind of water. Drink her water, and you would be thirsty again; drink his water, and you would never thirst again. Her water was external, taken in from the outside; his water was internal, flowing out from the heart. Her water was only temporary, but his water was eternal. Buckets were required to get her water; his water would be received by faith.   His water is life-changing water that catches us by surprise and overwhelms us with its force.

That's the way it was for this woman. In a single conversation in the heat of the day, she progressively recognized Jesus as a Jewish man (v. 9), as perhaps one greater than Jacob (v. 12), as a prophet (v. 19), and ultimately as the Messiah (vv. 25-26). He knew her every step, every choice, and every sin. In fact, it was his knowledge of her past that convinced her that this unexpected "somebody" really was Somebody.

Don't miss what the woman did next. She was so excited that she left her water pot behind (after all, she had found the living water), and she returned to the town that had rejected her to tell them about Jesus. That's what happens when we meet Jesus and are amazed by him: we go to tell others, including those who have turned against us. The woman who wanted to meet nobody couldn't wait to tell somebody what had happened at the well.

Look, though, at her evangelistic strategy: "Come, see a man who told me everything I ever did!" Give this some thought – have you ever seen an evangelistic tract that began this way?

Would this strategy attract you to Jesus? If you knew you could meet a man who knows *everything you ever did*, would you run to meet him? Might you want to meet him only in private, so no others would know your sin? I think I'd be hesitant to go at all.

That was not the case with the Samaritans, though. Many left their town to meet Jesus, and many believed in him because of this woman's witness. Many others then believed after they had heard Jesus himself. "Come, see a man" evangelism worked quite well.

What was so attractive about that strategy? Sometimes the Bible records only portions of conversations – though what the Bible gives us is always what we need – and I suspect that's the case here. We cannot know for sure, but I wonder if the woman's witness sounded something like this: "I met a man at Jacob's well today, and he offered me a different kind of water. He said the water is living water, and I'll never thirst again. Then he told me to get my husband, and he already knew that I've been married five times. He knew all about me . . . my sin, my wrong, my life . . . and do you know what? He knew everything I've ever done, *and he gave me living water anyway.*"

"And he gave me living water *anyway.*" He surprised her with his presence, and he amazed her with his grace. That kind of love always catches us by surprise.

Meditate for a while on these thoughts. If you are a follower of Christ, God called you to him, knowing all that you had ever done. He saved you, knowing all that you would ever do. He knows your yesterdays, todays, and tomorrows. He knows all about you, *and he gives you living water anyway.*

In fact, he will love you forever and ever.

The country music singer would, of course, repeat this great news: "Forever and ever. Amen."

Go tell this surprising news to somebody.

Reflection Questions

1. Remember when you first felt overwhelmed by God's love. When was that in your life?
2. List some words that describe God's love for you. Then list some words that describe your love for Him.
3. God loves us, and we are to love him. Genuine love for Christ is marked by our obedience. On a scale of 1-10 (with 1 meaning "not obedient at all" and 10 meaning "fully obedient"), where is your life today? How much do you love Christ?

Great Commission Action Step: Take a note card with you throughout the day. Watch and listen for people whose hurting lives are in need of living water. Be courageous enough to ask them if you might pray for them, and record their name for your prayer list. Make plans to keep in touch with them.

Prayer: "Father, thank you for loving me with a surprising eternal love. Help me to love you in return. Amen."

Be Amazed at His Forgiving Grace

Text: Psalm 51:1-7, 1 John 1:9

"Be prepared to be amazed."

Just in the last week, I've seen that catch phrase in all kinds of settings. Be prepared to be amazed at "cozy little kittens for sale" and "a unique way to make money by software development." Be amazed at a home for sale at a great price. At a new CD. At a "hopping new computer game." At a student jazz band. At LeBron James. Or, my personal favorite: be prepared to be amazed by a new superhero who will soon arrive on the scene. Seriously—I think the web writer really believed what he wrote.

Is it possible that we throw around the term "amazed" so much that the word has lost its force? To be amazed is to be filled with the emotional impact of astonishment and wonder, often in a surprising way. "Dumbfounded," "staggered," and "taken aback" work as well. I'm not sure if we are often "staggered" by cozy kittens, computer games, jazz bands . . . or even LeBron James.

I know, though, that we really should be "taken aback" when we focus on Jesus. The Master over all humbled himself to become one of us. He died in our place, offering us living water even though he knows all about us. He loves us with an undying love. His love is probably most clearly seen in the biblical images of what God does when he forgives our sin. Pause briefly here to ask God to amaze you with these images, and then let's press ahead by studying the final passages for this week.

Genuinely appreciating these truths requires that we first remember again our condition apart from a relationship with Jesus. God detests sin, and yet all of us are sinners (Rom. 3:23). Not one of us is good enough to be safely in God's presence (Mark 10:18). Without Christ, we are dead in our sin (Eph. 2:1-3) and held in darkness (Col. 1:13). Nothing about us is amazing.

What God does for us through the death of Jesus, though, is nothing short of amazing. First, God puts our sin "behind his back" where he cannot see it (Isa. 38:17). He blots out our wrong, sweeping it away like a cloud and a mist (Isa. 43:25, 44:22). Just like the morning wind blows away the haze, God carries away our sin. He blots it out as if the writing were erased from a parchment.

Second, God remembers our sin no more. Listen to these remarkable words of God's "forgetfulness."

> "It is I who sweep away your transgressions for My own sake and remember your sins no more." (Isa. 43:25)

> "For I will forgive their wrongdoing and never again remember their sin." (Jer. 31:34)

> "For I will be merciful to their wrongdoing, and I will never again remember their sins." (Heb. 8:12)

> "I will never again remember their sins and their lawless acts." (Heb. 10:17)

God does not literally forget our sin, because He knows all things. What He does do instead is choose not to hold our sin against us once he's forgiven us. He will not resurrect it and punish us, as his Son already paid the price for our sin (1 Cor. 6:20). It is as if God has erased our sin from his divine memory.

Third, God separates us from our sin as far as the east is from the west (Psa. 103:12). In the ancient mind, the distance between the east and the west was incalculable; the east and the west *never* met. Jesus separated us from our sin when he became sin for us and gave us his righteousness in return (2 Cor. 5:21). The mystery of that transaction is nothing less than incredible!

Fourth, God casts our sins into the depth of the sea (Mic. 7:19) – where they cannot be reached. Just as God vanquished the Egyptians and cast them into the Red Sea (Exod. 14-15), he conquers our sin and puts it beyond reach. All of our sin drops to the bottom like a heavy stone cast into the sea.

Read the images again. When God forgives our sin, he metaphorically puts it out of sight, out of mind, and out of reach. Behind his back. Remembered no more. Separated as east is from west. Into the bottom of the sea. The Bible summarizes it this way: "He has not dealt with us as our sins deserve or repaid us according to our offenses" (Psa. 103:10).

Guilty sinners separated from their sin. That's great news!

In fact, it gets even better. When God forgives, our sins that were like scarlet or crimson – pictures that indicate guilt – become white like snow (Isa. 1:18). Somehow, through the death of Christ, God atones for our sins. He doesn't just mask our sin or cover it up; he completely cleanses us from the inside. You have read today that when we confess our sin, he is "faithful and righteous to forgive us our sins and to cleanse us from all unrighteousness" (1 John 1:9). We can cry out in faith with David the psalmist, "Wash me, and I will be whiter than snow"! (Psa. 51:7).

You might have already known many of the Bible passages in today's reading. Maybe you've studied some of these images before. Knowing the images, though, is not enough if you haven't let the Word move your heart.

Have you lost your wonder at God's forgiveness? Do you realize the personal significance of "He has not dealt with *me* as *my* sins deserve"?

Are you taking grace for granted?

Or, has the enemy dragged your sin from the bottom of the ocean so that you are still haunted by yesterday's wrongs?

If you are a Christian, God has taken the darkness of your sin, somehow cleansed it through his blood, and made you as pure as white snow.

Think about it . . . and be amazed.

Reflection Questions

1. Which of the images of God's forgiveness is most inspiring to you? Why?
2. Describe a time when you were most certain of God's forgiveness.
3. Is there someone you need to forgive as God has forgiven you? Make plans to do so.

Great Commission Action Step: Memorize one of the Bible verses from today's study. Within the next week, quote the verse to someone who needs God's forgiveness.

Prayer: "Father, I praise you for your forgiveness. Thank you for not treating me as my sins deserve. Amen."

Be Amazed That He Uses Us Anyway

Text: Mark 6-8, John 17:9-17

I love to read the stories of the disciples in the Gospels, yet perhaps for an unexpected reason. I'm grateful God calls unexpected people to lead his church, but that's not the primary reason I love these stories. It's encouraging to read about the struggles of the disciples, but that's not my first interest. Peter is one of my favorite New Testament characters . . . though still not the reason I run to these stories.

I love these stories because of what they tell us about Jesus. He's a God of grace who gives second and third (and fourth and fifth . . .) chances. His patience is beyond comprehension. Amazing, actually.

Walk with me through the Gospel of Mark to see his patience. In Mark 6, more than 5000 people listening to Jesus were hungry, and Jesus challenged his disciples to feed them (vv. 31-44). That wouldn't work, they thought. They didn't have the food or the money needed to buy   food. You might know the story—Jesus multiplied five loaves of bread and two fish, provided enough food plus leftovers for all the people, and showed his creative power. So magnificent was this miracle that all four of the Gospel writers tell the story.

In the next story in Mark, Jesus walked on water toward the disciples in a boat. That scared them, for they thought he was a ghost. When Jesus got in the boat with them, the wind ceased – and the disciples were amazed (have you heard that before?). What catches my attention is how Mark describes their wonder: "They were completely astounded, because they had not understood about the loaves. Instead, their hearts were hardened" (vv. 51-52). They should have recognized more about Jesus by his power displayed in the feeding, but they didn't understand yet. They failed to see him as the sovereign one who can multiply the fish he created and walk on the water he controls.

Some time later, another 4000+ hungry people were with Jesus (8:1-10). Again he challenged his disciples to meet the need. This time, they started with seven loaves of bread and a few fish among the crowd. Same Jesus in their presence, fewer people to feed, and more food at the beginning – the scene for a miracle was set.

They knew he could multiply food. They had seen him at work. He had multiplied five loaves and two fish to feed 5000+; surely he could feed 4000+ with more loaves and fish. We read the story with expectation, waiting to see the Master glorify himself again.

But, the disciples' first response was again to question how they could feed that many people with too little food. Maybe they had completely forgotten the feeding of the 5000, but I doubt it. How do you forget that kind of miracle? More likely, they forgot who was with them. They saw the problem rather than the problem solver. Deity was in their midst, but their thinking remained earthly. It happens, you know – we work hard to solve our own problems while the Miracle Worker living within us longs for us to understand him better. It's no surprise we lose our wonder of Jesus when we fail to focus on him.

Sometime later, the disciples were again in a boat (Mark 8:14-21). This time, they were stressed because they had not brought enough bread to eat. They had only one loaf to share among them.

Stop here, and read this line again: *they were stressed because they had not brought enough bread to eat.*

Wouldn't you hope they would understand more about Jesus by now? Too little bread is not a problem for the Savior. Never has been. Never will be. If he can feed more than 5000, and then more than 4000, he can feed his twelve disciples. He is powerful enough to feed the multitudes and personal enough to feed you and me.

Still, we forget. We challenge others to remember God's power, but we forget it when we're the ones with the need. The closer the need is to us, the harder it is to see God's sovereign, miraculous hand at work. The circumstances look bigger to us than does the God over the circumstances. I wonder if Jesus might ever ask us what he asked his disciples then, "Do you not yet understand?" At what point might he give up on us?

You know the answer. He does not give up on us, but not because we are so good. We would be fully deserving if he walked away. He doesn't give up on us, though, because he trusts his Father's work in us, just as he trusted his Father's work in his disciples:

I pray for them. I am not praying for the world but for those You have given Me, because they are Yours. Everything I have is Yours, and everything You have is Mine, and I have been glorified in them. I am no longer in the world, but they are in the world, and I am coming to You. Holy Father, protect them by Your name that You have given Me, so that they may be one as We are one. . . . I am not praying that You take them out of the world but that You protect them from the evil one. They are not of the world, as I am not of the world. Sanctify them by the truth; Your word is truth. (John 17: 9-11, 15-17)

Jesus knows that the story is not about us in the first place. The one who creates us is the one who saves us, protects us, sanctifies us, and glorifies himself through us. He who is worthy of all praise loves us in spite of our unworthiness. He remembers us even when we forget him.

He is the Somebody who still uses nobodies.

Reflection Questions

1. What lessons of spiritual growth have been hard for you to learn?

2. Think of a time when God was patient with you. Thank him now for his grace.
3. Have you given up on someone you're trying to reach for Christ? If so, do you think God has given up?

Great Commission Action Step: Think of a believer who has seemingly stopped attending church. Lovingly seek to invite him/her to fellowship again with God's people.

Prayer: "Father, you are incredibly gracious. Thank you for using me in spite of me."

Be a Nobody

"Let us give up our work, our thoughts, our plans, ourselves, our lives, our loved ones, our influence, our all, right into His hand, and then, when we have given all over to Him, there will be nothing left for us to be troubled about, or to make trouble about."

--Hudson Taylor, 19th century missionary

"It [taking up the Cross] implies a state of mind that is ready to forsake all things, and endure all things, for his sake. . . ."

--Charles Finney, 19th century evangelist

Be a Nobody: Let Go of Your Name

Text: Mark 5:21-34

Oprah. Elvis. Madonna. Cher. Tiger. Barack.

They are so famous that we know them by their first name only. In most cases, they have worked hard, climbed up the ladder of success, and achieved much. We may not agree with their policies or actions, but we can't deny their global fame. They have earned a name for themselves.

Maybe you are working hard to achieve a name for yourself as well. If so, today's study will likely stretch you beyond your comfort zone. That's okay, though, if it's the Word of God that stretches us.

We have read this woman's story before in this study. For twelve years, she suffered with some type of blood disease. Most likely, this disease was a menstrual problem, making her unclean in her culture. She would not have been welcomed in any public place. She could not have gathered among the worshippers in the synagogue, and she would not have been permitted to touch the rabbi.

For over a decade, she had gone to the doctors. Surely she hoped day after day that *this* doctor would have the cure, but no healing came. Surely she longed for the day when the bleeding would stop, yet that day did not come. Surely she dreamed of a time when she would be welcomed among the crowds; however, no such time would come. As we saw in a previous study, the repetition within the text makes clear her desperate condition:

> "[She] *had endured much* under many doctors. She *had spent everything* she had and *was not helped at all*. On the contrary, *she became worse.*" (Mark 5:26, emphasis added)

By now, this woman had had all that she could take. Do you know anyone today like this woman? Someone who has little reason to look forward with expectation? Anybody who has been through so much that she seemingly cannot take another step? If you do not know anyone like this, you just don't know enough people – all over the world are people who awakened today without hope. If truth be told, living next door to you might be someone who is very much like the woman with the blood disease.

Jesus was coming through this woman's town, though, and she would somehow get to him. Tossing aside all cultural prohibitions, she somehow snaked her way through the crowd to touch Jesus. Perhaps with a bit of superstition – but with enough genuine faith that Jesus would respond to her – she reached out to touch just the bottom of his garment.

Instantaneously, Jesus did what no physician had been able to do in twelve years. The Messiah healed her, restoring her broken body to health and her wounded soul to redemption. Never would she be the same after the Son of God called her out, proclaimed her his "daughter," and gave her eternal life.

What a story! We could simply camp there and think about this woman's victory for a while – but the story will not allow us to stay there. You see, there was another unnamed, only slightly mentioned person in this story, and to miss his/her role in the story is to miss something significant. Look at this section of the story again:

"Having heard about Jesus, she came behind him in the crowd and touched his robe." (Mark 5:27)

Do you see the unnamed "hero" in the text? Somewhere, somehow, this woman had heard something about Jesus. We don't know who spoke to her, nor do we know what she heard. Maybe someone said to her, "Jesus is coming, and I've heard that he can give sight to the blind. Perhaps he can help you, too." Maybe another said, "I understand that he can give ears to the deaf and legs to the lame. Why, I've even heard that he can raise the dead!" Whoever it was that spoke to this woman, she heard enough that she would risk all to get to this one named Jesus.

This unknown person likely took a risk to point a hurting woman to Jesus, who had already stirred up trouble among the religious leaders. The dramatic change in the woman, though, was unquestionably worth the risk. A diseased woman was now well. One unwelcomed among the crowds was now welcomed by the Son of God. An outcast was now proclaimed a daughter. A woman with a dying future now had renewed hope.

Everything had changed — and the witness received no credit! His (or her) name was not even included in the story. Have you ever wondered why that would be?

It's really quite simple: the gospel is about the one to whom we witness rather than about us as witnesses. The writer of Mark's gospel was more concerned about proclaiming the majesty of Jesus than he was about giving glory to the witness.

This truth raises questions that are difficult indeed. Am I willing to be a witness for Jesus even if the world never knows my name? Am I prepared to do whatever Jesus demands even if my name is never mentioned in a book or on a website? Am I ready to go to an unreached people group where I will serve Jesus in the midst of obscurity and anonymity?

Or, do I sometimes care so much about my own name's being remembered that I rob Jesus of his glory?

If you want to be a Great Commission Christian, you must lay your name down and lift up his name alone. You must be willing to be a nobody for Jesus.

Reflection Questions

1. Rate yourself on a scale from 1 to 7 where you believe you are today.

   1 – I am not concerned that my name be remembered.
   2
   3
   4 – I want to lift up Jesus, but I am prideful.
   5
   6
   7 – I am most concerned that Jesus' name be remembered.

2. List some areas where you know your ungodly pride may be evident.

3. By yourself or with your group, list some positive steps to "lay down your own name and lift up His name alone." The suggestions at the end of this chapter might help you get started.

Great Commission Action Step: Read your local newspaper, looking for stories of people around the globe whose lives are difficult. If their geographical location is new to you, learn where their country is.

Slow your own life down enough to sense their "touch," and pray for them.

Prayer: "Father, change my heart so that I long to point to you more than to myself. At the end of my life, may your name be remembered more than mine. Amen."

Letting Go of Self

1. Give God thanks and praise for any good accomplishment you have ever done; refocus on him as the source of all good acts.
2. Do something good for someone else, but do it anonymously.
3. Spend some time praying for others, without addressing any of your own wants.
4. Ask God to focus your heart on others more than self.

Be a Nobody: Get Over Your Achievements

Text: Philippians 3:4-6, 1 Timothy 1:12-17

How important are achievements to you? I thought about that question several years ago when I read *Time* magazine's "The 100 Most Influential People in the World." Recipients varied from singer Lady Gaga to U.S. President Barack Obama to Chinese rebel Han Han to golfer Phil Mickelson. In the list were politicians, businesspersons, soldiers, musicians-singers, economists, TV and stage personalities, humanitarians, comedians, writers, designers, restaurateurs, scientists, physicians, philanthropists, educators, philosophers, lawyers, sports personalities, and a firefighter. I suspect that among the list were those who claim Christianity, Islam, Buddhism, Hinduism, Atheism, or any number of other belief systems as their "religion."

Several thoughts come to mind as I read this list. I was first reminded that the world is much larger than my daily North Carolina world. Included among these influencers were representatives from the United States, Brazil, Taiwan, Japan, France, Palestine, West Africa, Turkey, India, China, Canada, Russia, Ukraine, South Africa, Burma, Iran, Iraq, and Yemen. The human race is much bigger than any of us—but our Great Commission mandate to get the gospel to this ever changing and always growing world remains (Matt. 28:18-20).

We must do the Great Commission because all human beings—regardless of their achievements—are still eternally lost without a relationship with Jesus Christ. People around the globe are doing good things like promoting progress in Africa and Haiti, standing against oppressive regimes, seeking cures for deadly diseases, advancing reforms in education, counseling and feeding the poor, and championing basic human rights. Such acts are certainly honorable and worthy of the attention of a major news magazine—but *they do not earn salvation.* That is, in all of our "goodness," we remain sinners in need of a Savior (Rom. 3:23).

If you have read today's Bible reading, you know how easy it would have been for the apostle Paul to depend upon his goodness and his achievements. In fact, he admitted that truth:

"If anyone else thinks he has grounds for confidence in the flesh, I have more: circumcised on the eighth day; of the nation of Israel, of the tribe of Benjamin, a Hebrew born of the Hebrews; as to the law, a Pharisee; as to zeal, persecuting the church; as to the righteousness that is in the law, blameless." (Phil 3:4b-6)

As if Paul were writing a resume for Jewish obedience, he stacked up his credentials for his readers. By birth, he was a Hebrew circumcised rightly on the eighth day. By achievement, he was a Pharisee committed to defending his religion and following the Law with great precision. He fought for the traditions of his fathers, excelling in his Judaism (Gal. 1:13-14). How many of us could claim to be as faithful to our Christian teachings and traditions?

But, look again at today's second Bible reading. The apostle who was more zealous in his religion than his contemporaries also said that he was a blasphemer, a murderer, an arrogant man. He was, he said, the worst of sinners. So, was he a religious zealot or a vile sinner?

Paul was, in fact, both. By the world's standards, he achieved much. He likely would have been a regular on the Jewish religious channels, and he surely would have been featured on the cover of the popular magazines. By God's standards, though, Paul was a sinner separated from his Creator. All of his goodness amounted to nothing; apart from the grace and mercy of God, he had no hope.

Behind this story was also a little known, seldom featured disciple named Ananias (Acts 9: 1-19). Paul (then known as Saul) was on his way to Damascus to arrest Christians when Jesus met him on the way, struck him down, confronted him, and commissioned him. At the same time, God appeared to Ananias and told him to meet Paul, lay hands on him, and restore his sight.

We should not be surprised that Ananias questioned this command; after all, who wouldn't have done the same when Saul was known as a murderer? Nevertheless, Ananias followed God's Word – and he was instrumental in the calling of the apostle to the Gentiles.

God used a little known disciple to set apart a religious zealot who became a mighty evangelist, yet who learned that his own achievements apart from Christ meant nothing. Somehow, that just seems right in God's economy. God uses nobodies to proclaim the gospel to people who think they are somebodies . . . who then learn that nothing they've done can earn God's grace. God's love overwhelms them in their brokenness, and somebodies turned nobodies learn they really matter to the eternal God. How does that happen? It never happens unless somebody first tells the amazing story of Jesus (Rom. 10:14).

Think about believers who daily make Christ known around the world. They are salt and light to a lost world (Matt. 5:13-16), telling the Good News without concern for worldly recognition. They faithfully serve God through their local church, pointing a lost world to Jesus. These believers will likely never be featured in a national magazine. For some, to paint their portrait across the cover of *Time* magazine might, in fact, be dangerous.

But, these nobodies are *truly* influencers whose efforts make a difference.

Their efforts will, in fact, change eternity – and that's the kind of achievement that really matters.

That's a Great Commission achievement.

Reflection Questions

1. List several of your achievements that others might consider significant.

2. Now, go back and quote Paul's words after each achievement stated above: "But everything that was a gain to me, I have considered to be a loss because of Christ. More than that, I also consider everything to be a loss in view of the surpassing value of knowing Jesus Christ my Lord" (Phil. 3:7-8a).

3. Think about your level of activity in your local church. Do you equate your religious "busyness" with genuine Great Commission influence? Ask God to keep you from making this mistake.

Great Commission Action Step: Whatever you do today, do it so that Jesus is honored. Following one of the suggestions in the sidebar yesterday, do something good for someone else today—but do it anonymously. Pray that somehow your act of kindness will later open a door to sharing the gospel.

Prayer: "Father, teach me that my human achievements mean little. Instead, let me live for you in such a way that my life has Great Commission influence. To Christ be the glory forever and ever. Amen."

Be a Nobody: Beware of Greatness

Text: Mark 9:14-37

Sometimes you have to read a Bible passage more than once simply because it's hard to believe what you just read. Today's Scripture is one of those texts for me.

Get the picture. A distraught father whose son was possessed by a demon brought his boy to Jesus' disciples. Under the demon's influence, the son could not speak, foamed at the mouth, and often threw himself into fire or water to destroy himself. From his childhood he had been in this condition, and nothing was changing. We have to believe that the father had sought for years to find any solution to his boy's tragic condition. Any caring father would have done the same.

Like the woman with the blood disease (Mark 5:21-27), the father must have heard that Jesus (and apparently his disciples) had power to heal. Just as it always happens in God's Great Commission plan, somebody told this father about Jesus. In desperation, he brought his son to Jesus' disciples – and the tragic words of a defeated father speaking to Jesus echo loudly from the pages of Scripture: "So I asked Your disciples to drive it out, but they couldn't."

"But they couldn't." It's hard to find more tragic words about God's followers when hurting people turn to them for help. God's power was available to them, but they somehow missed it. They had previously dealt successfully with demons (Mark 6:12-13), but not this time. In fact, we learn that his disciples were both faithless (v. 19) and prayerless (v. 29) even as they confronted the spirit that controlled the man's son. We can only hope that Jesus' words – "You unbelieving generation! How long will I be with you? How long must I put up with you?" – caught their attention, but the evidence suggests otherwise.

Sometime later, Jesus retreated with his disciples and taught them about his coming betrayal, death, and resurrection. Perhaps not surprisingly, the disciples did not fully understand what he was teaching. He had previously predicted his death and resurrection, and Simon Peter had aggressively rebuked him for such teaching (Mark 8:31-33). Their leader didn't "get it" before, and now the whole group still didn't fully get it.

Here's what is astounding, though. In the very next passage, these same disciples were debating over who was the greatest. Read it again, because we need to let this text sink in:

> "When He was in the house, He asked them, 'What were you arguing about on the way?' But they were silent, because on the way they had been arguing with one another about who was the greatest."

Say what? The disciples likely were clinging to a hope that Jesus would be a political king who would offer them a cabinet seat, but their misunderstanding only magnifies their arrogance. Cast out a demon? They couldn't do it. Comprehend Jesus' teaching about his death? They failed. Understand the nature of Jesus' kingdom? Not yet. Willingly follow Christ's model of service? Not even close.

And these men were arguing over who was the greatest in a kingdom they didn't even understand?

Yep. It almost forces you to read the text again to make sure you got it right the first time, doesn't it?

Let's not kid ourselves, though. We are not always that much different. Sometimes we love our positions of power in the church even when we know we lack the power of God in our own lives. We strive for teaching positions without recognizing our own unwillingness to learn. Lesson after repeated lesson, we still don't get it. Our pride keeps us from admitting our lack of understanding even while our powerlessness keeps us from being effective. In all of our supposed greatness, God help us if we come face-to-face with a demon.

If the biblical stories in today's readings have not yet given us sufficient pause, look at the striking contrast that Jesus next painted. Over against his arrogant, failing disciples was Jesus lovingly taking a child into his arms.

To understand this picture, we need to know a first-century view of children. Little ones were deemed less than full persons, given no status or rights. While often portrayed as innocent, they were also considered weak, vulnerable, and dependent. Some teachers even grouped them with slaves and the weak-minded.   No wonder, then, that Jesus' disciples at times tried to drive bothersome children from their Master's presence (Mark 10:13).

Jesus' love for children teaches us at least two truths. First, we are to willingly welcome those who are like children – those who are weak, needy, dependent, and helpless (Mark 9:37). The world may cast them aside, but Christ-followers cannot. We are to serve helpless people who can offer us nothing in return. Indeed, to welcome such a person is to welcome Christ himself.

Second, we are to be like children (Mark 10:13-16). With the simple humility and unwavering faith of a child, we come to him as helpless little ones trusting him for life. We crawl into his lap, and he clutches us to his chest with his eternal arms. There we learn that we are both undeniably dependent *and* deeply loved.

God's children are needy people who welcome other needy people. In his work, rank and prominence carry no weight. When we get that right, we'll recognize that "greatness" no longer matters.

When we get that right, we'll go whenever, wherever, to whomever, to tell others about Jesus who willingly calls us to himself.

Get that right, and you'll be closer to being a Great Commission Christian.

Reflection Questions

1. Define "greatness" as the world defines it.
2. Think about believers that you consider to be "great" followers of Christ. What characteristics best describe them?
3. Check any of the statements that describe you today.

    _____ I am not as dependent on Christ as I should be.

    _____ Sometimes I want to be great in the eyes of the world.

    _____ I am learning to trust God as a child trusts a parent.

    _____ I struggle reaching out to needy, hurting people.

    _____ I am willing to go whenever, wherever, and to whomever Jesus wants me to go.

Great Commission Action Step: Work with your church's children's minister to determine some ways to reach out to children from non-believing homes. Then, take the lead in implementing one of those ways.

Prayer: "Father, make me childlike in trusting you. Remind me to beware of greatness. Amen."

Be a Nobody: Be Honest about Your Sin

Text: Luke 22:31-62

I like adventure. Get me to whitewater rapids, and I want to run them. Show me a bungee cord, and my sense of adventure will trump my fear of heights. My firefighting training is certainly a product of my desire to help, but I cannot deny the thrill of a fire run. I like people who are willing to take a risk to learn, to grow, to help others.

That's why Simon Peter is one of my favorite Bible characters. He willingly left his fishing business at Jesus' command, not entirely knowing where that commitment would take him (Matt. 4:18-20).

When other disciples cowered during a storm on the sea, Peter risked walking on the water to be with Jesus (Matt. 14:22-29). Simon was one disciple willing to defend Jesus in the Garden of Gethsemane

(John 18:10-11) – though his fishing background apparently weakened his skills with a sword!

Unchecked risky living also sometimes leads to failure, however, and that certainly was the case with Peter. Re-read today's scripture reading, and watch the steps to Peter's collapse in denying Christ:

1. vv. 31-34 – Peter, although he certainly believed that he would die for Christ, was overconfident in his faithfulness to Christ. Jesus knew better, but Peter was not ready to hear. Our overconfidence often clouds the reality that all of us have the potential of denying Christ before the rooster crows in the morning.

2. vv. 39-46 – Emotional drain, physical weariness, and spiritual confusion caused Peter and the other disciples to sleep when they should have been praying. Prayerlessness is always a step in the wrong direction.

3. vv. 47-53 – Overconfidence plus prayerlessness often leads to our trying to solve problems in our own power and according to our own plans. That's what Peter did when he took out a sword.

4. vv. 54-55 – Give Peter credit for still following Jesus, but he also found himself sitting among the enemies. Sitting in the wrong place with the wrong people at the wrong time is never a healthy sign for Jesus' followers. That happens, though, when we trust in ourselves and let our guard down.

5. vv. 56-60 – The fall came when Peter, by his words and his actions, denied knowing Jesus. Not only did he deny Christ once, but his sin quickly snowballed when he committed the same act two more times. It's frightening how steep the drop is once we have made the decision to go down the wrong side.

And then, just as Jesus had warned, the rooster crowed. In fact, the rooster crowed even while Peter was still speaking his third denial. Look closely at the next verse, though. Dwell on it for a minute, allowing the picture to be painted in your mind:

"Then the Lord turned and looked at Peter."
(v. 61)

Wow – that's halting. Jesus was under arrest, heading toward a cross. Peter was attempting to blend in with the enemies, even verbally denying his commitment to Christ. In the midst of Peter's denials, the Lord himself turned and looked at Peter. Face to face. Eyeball to eyeball. Heart to heart. Loving Lord to denying disciple.

Peter would learn in a painful way just how far down his sin would take him. The committed disciple who had said he would die for Jesus now would not even admit his relationship with Christ. The one who had walked on the water to be with Jesus now did his best to walk away from him. The tough fisherman had become a shrinking coward, revealing his spinelessness more with every word that he spoke.

But – and here's another reason to be amazed at Jesus – Peter would also learn that he could not fall so far that Jesus couldn't see him. Jesus never took his eyes off his disciple even in the midst of denial. His piercing look of grace overshadowed the fleeing heart of Peter. The Lord's look, combined with the reminder of the rooster's crowing, melted the tough fisherman. All Peter could do was weep bitterly.

The story does not end there, though. On resurrection morning, an angel that met the women at the tomb told them to tell the good news to Jesus' disciples *and Peter* (Mark 16:7) – as if to say, "Don't forget that Peter is still one of them, too." Peter's fall did not ultimately break his relationship with Jesus; the Lord whom he denied would not deny him. Indeed, Jesus would later challenge Peter to be a shepherd set apart to feed his sheep (John 21:15-17).

What amazing grace is evident when a fallen fisherman is not only restored, but is also set apart to teach God's Word! Here's the point – *Peter was most ready to tell the good news after he had fallen and been forgiven, for only then was he most ready to speak of grace.*

Does that mean we should intentionally sin so that we can appreciate grace? Of course not. God forbid that we should think that way (Rom. 6:2). Instead, we simply need to recognize our sin, grieve over it, turn from it, and appreciate God's amazing grace again. Should God bring us to weeping bitterly over our sin to get us there, so be it.

Are you willing to admit every sin of your life, realizing that God already knows what you're doing? Are you ready to be so cleansed that you cannot help but tell others about God's grace?

Go ahead, take the risk. You haven't fallen so far that Jesus doesn't know where you are.

Reflection Questions

1. In the steps of Peter's fall, where do you most often find yourself?
2. Define "grace" as you understand it. When was the last time that you told somebody about the power of God's grace in your life?
3. What steps can you take to avoid a fall? Maybe the steps below will help you.

<u>Countering a Fall</u>

1. Admit your dependence on God.
2. Pray without ceasing.
3. Seek God's wisdom every day.
4. Be aware of first steps in the wrong direction. Stop there.
5. If you fall, immediately admit your sin and turn back to God.

Great Commission Action Step: Using the prayer below, spend time allowing God to point out the sin in your life. Allow the Spirit of God to cleanse you so you give evidence of Christian integrity. His forgiveness will again make you want to speak about him.

Prayer: "Father, show me my sin, and then let me live in your grace. Make your grace amazingly real to me. Amen."

Be a Nobody: Be Willing to be Broken

Text: 2 Corinthians 12:1-10

Cedar Point Amusement Park in Ohio is known for its roller coasters. "Millennium Force," probably the best known coaster in the park, broke ten world records when it opened in 2000. The Raptor is an inverted coaster with six head over heels inversions in less than a mile. The "Top Thrill Dragster" is one of the highest roller coasters in the world. Rising over 400 feet into the air, this coaster launches riders from 0 to 120 miles per hour in less than four seconds. If these rides aren't enough, you might try one of the other fourteen coasters in the park.

Spend the day at Cedar Point, and you will experience ups, downs, upside-downs, and inside-outs – all in the name of fun. But, do you know what most strikes me about roller coasters? Were there no "downs," the trip would be no fun. The journey up is exciting, but only because we know that the trip down is still to come. Hands in the air, face forward, heading straight into the ground at breakneck speeds – that's why we ride coasters!

We don't think that way about life, though, do we? We like the ups, but the downs aren't so much fun. We like the view from the top, but seldom do we rejoice in the downs.

Compare that thinking to the Apostle Paul's story in today's Bible passage. This passage sounds much like a roller coaster ride: way up (a marvelous vision), way down (a painful thorn), and way up again (deep rejoicing). The way down and the second "way up," however, make little sense to us. So, fasten your seat belt, and prepare for this challenge to be a nobody for Jesus.

The experience was first a tremendous one for Paul. It must have been, as he spoke of it in the third person and could find no words to adequately describe it. To be honest, we learn little about his experience, except that Paul was taken up into the heavens. He was not sure how it happened, and he could not repeat the words that he heard. Whatever happened to Paul, God had a divine purpose. The experience must have been for Paul an "up" like few other ups.

To keep Paul from becoming arrogant, though, God allowed the enemy to torment him through a thorn in the flesh. Paul's vision of heaven stirred up the demons of hell, and they attacked with full force. The wording suggests that the thorn, whatever it was, was severe. It was bad enough that Paul pleaded with God multiple times to remove it – but God would not. Even for the apostle extraordinaire, God said no, choosing instead to teach Paul that, "'My grace is sufficient for you, for power is perfected in weakness.'" At least temporarily, this must have been for Paul a serious "down" on the roller coaster ride.

Here, God turns the world's thinking upside down. Power is usually the product of training, of discipline, of position and authority – not of weakness. His power, though, is available to us not when we are strongest, but when we're weakest. In fact, the Bible is filled with stories of God's using weakness to accomplish his plan by showing his power. Think about these few examples.

1. Moses said he was "'slow and hesitant in speech,'" but God told him that he would help him speak and teach him what to say (Exod. 4:10-12).

2. God systematically reduced Gideon's army so they would know that he alone had delivered them (Judges 7:1-25).

3. David had only a sling and rock, but God directed the rock to take down the Philistine giant (1 Sam. 17:1-50).

4. Jeremiah said he was only a child, yct God promised to go with him (Jer. 1:7-8).

5. More than once, God reminded his people that the battle was his, not theirs (Exod. 14:13-14, 1 Sam. 17:47, 2 Chron. 20:17).

For Paul, the weakness created by the thorn in his flesh caused him to depend more on God for strength. He learned so much in that experience that he concluded, "I will most gladly boast all the more about my weaknesses, so that Christ's power may reside in me" (2 Cor. 12:9). In his anguish, Paul experienced strength in God's presence; in his weakness, he found power. The more that God allowed a "down" in Paul's life, the more the apostle experienced God.

Here is where the Great Commission intersects with our brokenness. The message of the gospel is always glorious, whether we're experiencing the mountaintop or the valley. The world takes note, however, when we can still speak of joy even when life is tough. To gladly boast about weakness makes little sense, but it surely witnesses to the presence of God within us. Somehow, the "down" of the roller coaster turns upward; the peace that Christ gives us in our brokenness really is beyond understanding (Phil. 4:7)

For the sake of a world that needs Jesus, are you willing to pray, "Lord, make me weak so I might always depend on you"? Pray that way, and God may allow the enemy to have direct access to your life. Your family and friends may not understand where God is in the midst of your struggles. He might orchestrate the events of life to keep you humble. When God breaks us, though, we are no longer focused on self. We're no longer interested in being somebody. We seek only his grace that is sufficient for every struggle.

When that happens, the world sees something uniquely powerful in the gospel. The good news spreads, and Jesus' name is magnified.

We are weakened for Christ's sake, broken by his grace.

And that's a good place to be. A nobody for Jesus.

Reflection Questions

1. What is your response to the concept of brokenness?
2. Do you believe that brokenness might be an expression of God's love for you?
3. How has God used the circumstances of life to break you in the past? How might he be breaking you today?

Great Commission Action Step: Begin to look for ways to connect with people outside of your church. Join a local community organization. Coach in a local little league. Get connected, and you will likely find broken people who need Jesus.

Prayer: "Father, I want to be in a place where you can best use me. Do what you must to make me a nobody for your glory. Amen."

Be a Nobody: Give Up Self for Non-Believers

Text: Romans 9:1-3

I want to introduce you to some of my friends today. My African friend still sacrifices animals to appease his perceived gods. He believes that if the gods are angry, his child might get sick or his crops might fail. I don't agree with his view, but I grew to appreciate his friendship during a trip to the African continent.

My friend in the Pacific Rim is a Buddhist. I met him when he taxied us around a major urban center in Thailand. Despite our language differences, he helped me to understand more about his religion. I don't comprehend his use of Buddha statues, yet I found him to be respectful and caring.

I met my Muslim friend while teaching an English class in another part of the world. Our discussions about our respective faiths were fascinating and enlightening for both of us. We learned from each other, though neither of us convinced the other.

My friend Scott is a trainer I worked out with several years ago. He was committed to physical health but less interested in spiritual matters. He wasn't opposed to discussions, though; he was just ignorant about the subject. Nowhere in his life had he been exposed to the gospel.

Because I care about all of these men, I want them to know Jesus Christ as Savior and Lord. Hell is real, and I don't want them to spend eternity under God's judgment. How exciting it would be to join them among the nations, tribes, tongues, and people who will worship God eternally (Rev. 5:9)! I do want them to be saved.

I need to be honest, though. What I don't know is *how much* I want them to be saved. Would I echo Paul's words as he spoke about his Jewish friends, "I speak the truth in Christ—I am not lying; my conscience is testifying to me with the Holy Spirit—that I have intense sorrow and continual anguish in my heart. For I could almost wish to be cursed and cut off from the Messiah for the benefit of my brothers, my own flesh and blood" (Rom. 9:1-3)?

Would I be willing to be accursed so others can know Jesus?

To be candid, Paul's words make me uncomfortable. He spoke truth that would be hard for me to speak. The Jesus who is truth (John 14:6) would confirm there was no lie in Paul's speech. Then, the Holy Spirit in him bore witness that Paul spoke with a pure conscience. There was no guile in his words. He genuinely bore great sorrow and non-stop anguish because the Jews had not turned to Christ.

Paul so grieved their lostness that if it were possible, he would be willing to be separated from Christ – to suffer God's judgment in their place – for them to be saved. He knew, of course, that was impossible, as nothing could separate him from the love of God (Rom. 8:31-39). That truth surely only added to his grief, though. He was willing to give himself up, but that was not an option. He loved a people even his sacrificial willingness could not save.

Remember his history, though, that we studied earlier. Prior to his conversion, Paul was advanced in Judaism beyond others (Gal. 1:14). He was of the tribe of Benjamin, a Hebrew of the Hebrews, a zealous Pharisee who lived blamelessly according to the Law (Phil. 3:5-6). His teacher had been Gamaliel, the most prominent rabbi of his day (Acts 22:3). Religious leaders had given him authority to persecute the growing sect of Christians, and he carried out that role with vigor.

His was a resume worth bragging over to an extent. The Jewish leaders empowered him, and the early church feared him. Like him or not, Paul was a somebody before he met Christ.

And then God supernaturally struck him down with a light, saved him from his sin, and set him apart as an apostle extraordinaire to take the gospel to the Gentiles (Acts 9). The persecuting zealot became the gospel-preaching zealot. In our world, the apostle Paul would likely be invited to our evangelical platforms. His books would sell, and his website would be frequently visited. He would still be a somebody . . . but he would be willing to give it all up so people might know Christ.

Indeed, he would suffer punishment on their behalf if doing so would save them. He was willing to become a nobody – to be cursed like a common criminal – because he so loved unbelieving people.

He wanted others to know Christ more than he wanted them to know him.

So much keeps me from going there sometimes. I like recognition. I'm more comfortable hanging around believers than I am developing relationships with non-believers. I hope my books sell well. I want my students to love and respect me. In an odd twist, I occasionally speak too publicly about what I've done behind the scenes to help others. To be willing to be accursed for others is a stretch for me even as I write these words.

Frankly, I'd rather people get saved without costing me much. I want others to join me in heaven – not replace me there.

My heart can wander so far from the heart of Christ, who loved me enough to die for me while I was yet a sinner (Rom. 5:8). He endured the world's ridicule to save me from my arrogance. He took upon himself the form of a servant so I might be his beloved child (Phil. 2:7).

He was, in the view of his neighbors, a nobody, just the son of a carpenter (Matt. 13:55). Yet he was so much more than that. He was the Son of God who chose to be accursed in our place.

For me he did that. For you. For my friends I introduced to you at the beginning of this chapter. And for the billions of people I don't know, and who don't know me. Would I be willing to be cursed for them so they might know Jesus?

God, please make me willing to be a nobody for others' sake.

Reflection Questions

1. Would you be willing to be cursed so others might be saved?
2. In what area of your life do you struggle with pride?
3. Be honest – for what are you living?

Great Commission Action Step: Spend some time learning about unreached people groups at www.joshuaproject.net. Ask God to break your heart even over people you don't know.

Prayer: "Father, I need your help to love people so much I would give myself up for them. Give me that kind of burden for others."

Do Something

"Rest in this - it is His business to lead, command, impel, send, call or whatever you want to call it. It is your business to obey, follow, move, respond, or what have you."

--Jim Elliott, 20th century missionary

"Lord, whatever you want, wherever you want it, and whenever you want it, that's what I want."

--Richard Baxter, 17th century pastor

Do Something: Pray "God's Heart" for the World

Text: Romans 10:1

Let's go back to the introduction of this study. You might remember one of my primary concerns: we are attempting to programmatically create Great Commission Christians out of believers who've lost their awe of God and have built their own kingdoms in the process. The goal of this study has been to restore our wonder while making us willing to be nobodies for God's glory.

If all we do is theologize, however, we haven't done enough. Somewhere, we must start *doing something*. Each day's action step has been a practical starting point for this process. These final two studies take us to the most basic steps toward living a Great Commission lifestyle: praying and proclaiming. I realize neither of these "secrets" is a surprise to you, but that's precisely the point. People who are amazed by God will do both.

Three years before my father passed away, he turned to Christ for salvation. It was quite a miracle, actually. My dad had quite a temper prior to his conversion. My childhood memories of his displays of anger still echo in my mind. Though my grandmother was a strong believer, Dad never showed interest in Christianity. In fact, he first believed that many routes lead to God; "we're just following different paths," he told me.

We prayed for more than 30 years that Dad would become a believer. Then, it happened. Dad called my little brother to say he wanted to talk about following Jesus . . . right then! God so transformed my father that we spent the final years of his life getting to know a new man. He was a trophy of God's grace, an undeniable example of 2 Corinthians 5:17a—"Therefore, if anyone is in Christ, he is a new creation." God graciously answered our prayers.

The Apostle Paul so deeply longed for his people to follow Christ that this was his "heart's desire and prayer to God" (Rom. 10:1). The urgency of the moment and his genuine love for others motivated his praying from the depth of his being. Nobodies for Jesus intercede that way on behalf of others. They understand that Great Commission living is based on Great Commission praying.

Are you praying for non-Christians to turn to Christ? In my book, *Serving in Your Church Prayer Ministry* (Zondervan), I describe a simple way to pray evangelistically by praying the acronym, "GOD'S HEART." I'm grateful to my friend Chris Schofield, whose writings about prayer first helped me to think about this kind of process. Maybe this pattern will help you as you pray evangelistically for others:

G = Pray believers, beginning with yourself, will appreciate **God's grace**. When we really appreciate what God has done for us, we naturally want to tell others about Him. That's why new believers are often most willing to do evangelism—their salvation is so fresh they almost can't avoid telling the story. We stop evangelizing when we take grace for granted.

O = Pray for believers to live in **obedience** to God. We can't change another person's heart. Only God can do that, as he did in response to our prayers for my dad. If we're not walking in obedience to God, though, our disobedience hinders our prayers (Isa. 59:1-2). Abiding in Christ really does matter when we pray (John 15:7).

D' = Pray believers will *decide* to tell others. Evangelism doesn't just happen. Telling the story of Jesus is a choice . . . an action . . . a decision. Too many Christians know they should do evangelism, but decide not to do it. Pray that won't happen in your life.

S = Pray that believers will *speak* the gospel fearlessly and clearly. In fact, that's the way Paul taught us to pray in Ephesians 6:19-20 and Colossians 4:2-4. If Paul – the apostle extraordinaire – needed others praying for him to do evangelism, how much more do we need that kind of support? Enlist someone to pray this way for you.

H = Pray for nonbelievers to have a receptive *heart* to the gospel. Apart from Christ, all people are dead in their sin (Eph. 2:1), held under the devil's sway (Acts 26:18). Only God can make their hearts open to the good news.

E = Pray their spiritual *eyes* will be opened. Non-believers are blinded to the truth of the gospel (2 Cor. 4:3-4), and the "god of this age" does all he can to keep them in darkness. Nothing we do apart from the power of God can open their blinded minds.

A = Pray they will have God's **attitude** toward sin. Understanding God's remedy for sin begins with understanding our sickness. We're all sinners (Rom. 3:23), and we must see our sin as God sees it – as wrong against a holy God.

R = Pray non-believers will **repent** and believe. The message of Christ is clear: we must turn from our sin and trust Christ for salvation (Mark 1:15). God gets the glory as he frees nonbelievers from the domain of darkness (Col. 1:13).

T = Pray their lives will be **transformed**. Only God can change a man like he changed my dad. Here's the good news, though – he's still doing that! When God does that, the non-believing world takes note.

Who is praying for you to speak the gospel boldly and clearly? Are you praying for other believers to be evangelistic? Are you praying for non-believers? Are you asking God to save and transform a specific person? Are you praying for a people group that has never heard the name of Jesus?

A Great Commission lifestyle begins on our knees. We walk this journey on our knees. It ends on our knees, when we will bow before God throughout eternity. If your prayers have focused more on self than others, change that pattern today. Start right now by praying for someone who does not know Christ.

If you've already been praying for someone for many years, don't give up. God is still a miracle working God who responds to the prayers of his people. He still hears nobodies.

That's his heart. And that's still amazing.

Reflection Questions

1. Who prayed for you to become a believer?
2. How strong has been your focus on praying for others to follow Christ?
3. For whom will you begin praying today? What specific person? What specific people group?

Great Commission Action Step: Review the websites of the Southern Baptist Convention's International Mission Board (www.imb.org) and the North American Mission Board (www.namb.net). Begin to pray for people whose stories you learn there.

Prayer: "Father, give me your heart for others. Make prayer a part of my DNA rather than just a ritual."

Do Something: Tell Your Story

Text: Acts 26:4-18

We make evangelism way too hard.

I realized this truth almost accidentally while my future wife and I were dating. I was a single pastor, and my church always got far more excited than I did when I was dating someone. Almost delirious, in fact. Because of that, Pam and I decided not to tell people in our respective churches that we were dating. We wanted some privacy as we were figuring out God's plan for our lives.

It didn't take long, though, for our church members to find out what was happening – like, only a few hours, it seemed! Word got out and then spread like a wildfire.

"The preacher's dating somebody."
"I hear she's really a good girl."
"Wonder where they met?"
"Has he brought her to church yet?"

"I thought I saw him with someone at the restaurant!"

Do you know how our churches learned about our relationship? It's probably not surprising: we told them. Pam told her best friend, "Now, don't tell anybody yet, but I'm dating someone." I told my favorite deacon, "I need to trust with this, but I've got to tell somebody. I really like this girl." Pam and I agreed we'd tell nobody, but we quickly broke our word. We just had to tell somebody.

That's been the theme of this entire study. When you fall in love with someone who amazes you, you talk. You don't keep quiet when somebody's love for you gives you significance and meaning. It's as if you just can't keep the good news to yourself. Like a volcano that breaks out of its confines, the gospel erupts from a changed heart. Even the heart of a nobody.

Actually, *especially* the heart of a nobody.

You see, nobodies don't have to have all the answers. They just need to know THE answer.

Nobodies don't have to be preachers. They need only to be Christians.

Nobodies don't have to have training, though training is good. They only have to have a story. Their story, written by God.

Nobodies don't strive for fame. They are consumed only by talking about Jesus.

Nobodies aren't worried about living. They are willing to die for the sake of others.

They tell the story of Jesus because they are nobodies overwhelmed by the love of their Creator. It's as if they can't help it.

Think again about the story of the man possessed by demons in Mark 5:1-20, where we started this study together. He must have been a frightening sight, living naked among the tombs. He was shackled by chains, but he broke his bonds. Night and day he screamed. He cut himself with stones, perhaps attempting to end his misery. The demons inside him were so many that his name was "Legion," a word referring to a large unit of the Roman army.

I can only imagine what the townspeople thought about him. "Stay away from the graveyard," the mothers must have said. "The crazy man's there." Generations might have heard about their previous unsuccessful attempts to bind him: "I've heard that he's broken the chains again. I don't know what we're going to do." The incessant screams echoing through the night must have frightened even the strongest men. Only the demons wanted to be near this nobody in the cemetery.

Until Jesus showed up, that is. When he showed up, the world changed. The demons knew their reign in this man was over. They were no match for the one they recognized as the Son of the Most High God.

The change in this man was striking, in fact. The crazy man became sane. The naked man was clothed. His screams of demonic control would be replaced with shouts of praise. So dramatic was his change that the townspeople were frightened when they say him. After all, Jesus had done something amazing in his life.

This man did what you and I would likely do: ask to stay with Jesus, who had changed him remarkably. That wasn't Jesus' plan, though. He doesn't work miracles in our lives so we can just hang out with him. He changes us so we can proclaim his power and grace to others. "Go back home to your own people, and report to them how much the Lord has done for you and how He has had mercy on you," Jesus told the man (Mark 5:19).

Can you see it? Can you hear him? Can you hear his people as they see him from a distance?

> "That looks like him, but I don't know. He looks different."
> "No, that's him. Something's happened to him."
> "Be careful. Remember, he has demons."
> "I don't know exactly what happened," he answers. "But I do know this: Jesus came by. He spoke, and the demons left. I know I'm not afraid anymore. I don't want to die anymore. You need to meet this Jesus. He's incredible."

The result? People throughout the ten cities of the Decapolis were amazed at Jesus (Mark 5:20). Evangelism really is that easy.

Let me make the point one more time: that's the way it's supposed to work. A nobody amazed by Jesus tells everybody what Jesus did, and others then marvel in turn. The gospel erupting from us leads to changed lives.

You, too, have a story to tell if you're a Christ follower. You know who you were, and you know how God changed you. You know what he means to you today. If you're taking him for granted, ask God to restore your wonder. Become a child again who is amazed by the mercy of God.

Then, do something with your story.

Go tell somebody.

And don't worry if you're a nobody. That's who God wants you to be.

Reflection Questions

1. As you complete this study, which of the following statements best describes you? Check all that fit.

    _____ I'm afraid I'm still not amazed by Jesus.

    _____ I am so amazed at Jesus that I'm ready to go anywhere to tell others about him.

    _____ My wonder in Jesus is increasing.

2. If you were to tell your story to someone today, who would that person likely be?
3. What most amazes you about Jesus today?

Great Commission Action Step: Go back to the basics. Do something with the Great Commission – tell your story to somebody.

Prayer: "Father, thank you for being so amazing. Increase my wonder everyday so I might tell others. Like John the Baptist, I must decrease, and you must increase."

Telling Your Story

Following Paul's example in Acts 26:5-18, tell somebody your story:

1. What my life was like before meeting Christ.
2. How I knew I needed to follow Christ.
3. How I came to know Christ.
4. What my life has been like since meeting Christ.

Conclusion

As I finish this book, I am reminded again about what I hope this book accomplishes. If it brings me honor, I will have somehow moved you in an erroneous direction. If it leads you to do something to gain fame, I will have done something wrong. Anything less than pointing you, the reader, and others to Jesus will have missed my objective.

Here's what I want to happen. My prayer is that God will use you to speak to somebody about our Savior, the Lord Jesus Christ. I pray you will speak of his wonder, and he will so work through you that you can't help but speak of him again. I long to know that someone will worship him around his throne because you have talked about how amazing Christ is. He alone is worthy of our praise.

Thank you, friend, for joining me in this journey. Perhaps I will meet you this side of heaven, but perhaps not. If not, that's okay.

The story is not about us anyway.

9488230R00062

Made in the USA
San Bernardino, CA
18 March 2014